# SPACE TRAVEL

Patricia Whitehouse

Heinemann Library
Chicago, Illinois

Designed by Heinemann Library
Printed in China by South China Printing.

08 07 06 05 04
10 9 8 7 6 5 4 3 2 1

**Library of Congress Cataloging-in-Publication Data**

Whitehouse, Patricia, 1958-
  Space travel / Patricia Whitehouse.
    v. cm. -- (Space explorer)
  Includes bibliographical references and index.
  Contents: Going to space -- Rockets for space travel -- Is space safe for people? -- First person in space -- Early space missions -- Next stop: the Moon -- One small step for man... -- Traveling on the Moon -- A problem in space -- Space shuttle -- Space stations -- Missions to other planets -- Space elevators and other ways to travel -- Amazing space facts.
  ISBN 1-4034-5155-9 (Library Binding-hardcover) -- ISBN 1-4034-5659-3 (Paperback)
  1.  Astronautics--Juvenile literature. 2.  Space travel--Juvenile literature. 3.  Outer space--Exploration--Juvenile literature. [1. Astronautics. 2. Space travel. 3. Outer space--Exploration.] I. Title. II. Series.
  TL793.W4923 2004
  910'.919--dc22
                                    2003026766

**Acknowledgments**
The author and publishers are grateful to the following for permission to reproduce copyright material:

Cover photograph: Science Photo Library.
p. 4 Bettmann/Corbis; Getty Images; p. 5 NASA;
p. 6 NASA; p. 7 Getty Images; p. 8 KPT Power Photos;
p. 9 Getty Images; p. 10 Getty Images; p. 11 Getty Images; p. 12 NASA; p. 13 NASA; p. 14 Science Photo Library; p. 15 Science Photo Library; p. 16 NASA;
p. 17 Science Photo Library; p. 18 NASA; p. 19 NASA;
p. 20 NASA; p. 21 NASA; p. 22 Science Photo Library;
p. 23 NASA/Science Photo Library; p. 24 Getty Images/ Photodisc; p. 25 NASA; p. 26 Getty Images/ Photodisc;
p. 27 NASA; p. 28 NASA; p. 29 NASA/Science Photo Library

Every effort has been made to contact copyright holders of any material reproduced in this book. Any omissions will be rectified in subsequent printings if notice is given to the publisher.

Special thanks to Geza Gyuk of the Adler Planetarium for his comments in preparation of this book.

Some words are shown in bold, **like this.** You can find out what they mean by looking in the glossary.

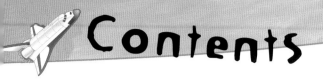

# Contents

# Going to Space

On October 4, 1957, the **Soviet Union** launched a rocket into space. The rocket was carrying a **satellite** called Sputnik. This was the first time anything had been sent into space.

**Life-size models of the satellite Sputnik were shown around the world.**

A lot of rocket design and experiments had to be done before people could go into space.

For 21 days, Sputnik sent its "beep beep" radio signal to Earth. It was a success. People started thinking about sending a person to space.

# Making Rockets

Sending a **satellite** into space was not easy. The Earth's **gravity** pulls everything toward Earth's center. Scientists had to make a rocket that could break free from Earth's gravity.

The scientist Robert Goddard with his rocket in 1926.

Scientists worked on many different rocket designs. After many **experiments,** rockets could finally escape Earth's gravity.

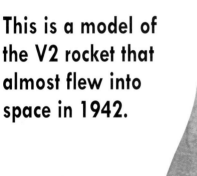

This is a model of the V2 rocket that almost flew into space in 1942.

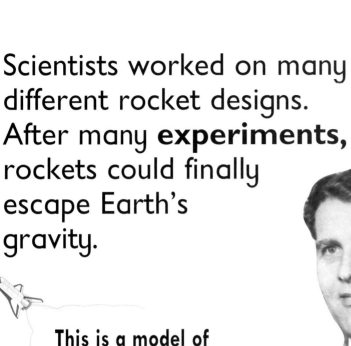

# Is Space Safe for People?

After 1957, rockets could fly into space. But no one knew if it was safe for a living thing to go into space. Could it survive a rocket launch? Would space make it sick?

**Being in space or on the Moon is very different from being on Earth.**

On November 3, 1957, a dog named Laika became the first living thing to go into space. This helped scientists learn about making space travel safe for people.

# First Person in Space

On April 12, 1961, the spacecraft Vostok 1 was launched. A **Soviet cosmonaut** named Yuri Gagarin was in it. He became the first person to go into space.

The Vostok 1 flight was controlled by computers on Earth. As Vostok 1 came back to Earth, Gagarin was ejected from the spacecraft and landed by parachute. His flight had lasted only 108 minutes.

Yuri Gagarin became a hero when he landed back on Earth.

On May 5, 1961, U.S. **astronaut** Alan Shepard became the second person to go into space. His spacecraft was called Freedom 7. This time, Shepard controlled the spacecraft himself.

The **capsules** of the first space missions were tiny. Shepard stayed inside his space capsule when he returned to Earth. It landed in the sea.

capsule

Early space capsules had just enough room for a seat and controls.

**To get ready for going to the Moon, astronauts practiced landing vehicles on Earth.**

Once people could get to space, the next challenge was to land on the Moon. **Astronauts** began some difficult training for Moon missions.

14

Engineers worked on designing
safe space shuttles.

The **Soviet Union** and the United
States both wanted to be the first to
send a person to the Moon. Scientists
and engineers in both countries worked
on plans and built equipment. Finally,
the first Moon mission was ready.

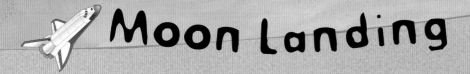

# Moon Landing

U.S. **astronauts** Michael Collins, Buzz Aldrin, and Neil Armstrong left Earth on July 16, 1969. They traveled for four days and covered over 210,000 miles (350,000 kilometers).

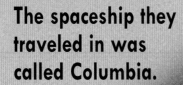

The spaceship they traveled in was called Columbia.

When Neil Armstrong first stepped onto the
Moon he said, "That's one small step for a
man, one giant leap for mankind."

Neil Armstrong and Buzz Aldrin boarded
a **lunar module.** It left Columbia and
landed on the Moon. Armstrong was the
first person to step onto the Moon.

# Traveling on the Moon

On the first three Moon landings, **astronauts** explored the Moon on foot. They could not go very far from their **lunar module.**

Astronauts collected rock and dust samples from the Moon.

On the fourth mission to land on the Moon, astronauts took a **Lunar Roving Vehicle.** They could now explore places farther away.

19

# A Problem in Space

Scientists work hard to make sure each space flight is safe. But sometimes things go wrong. On the Apollo 13 mission to the Moon, a tank exploded.

Scientists check all the equipment that will go into space, but something could still go wrong.

Before the Apollo 13 mission, the crew had trained hard to be ready to go into space.

The **astronauts** on Apollo 13 were running out of air and water. For four days, Mission Control worked hard to help the astronauts get back to Earth safely.

People wanted to send more **astronauts** and equipment on each mission. Scientists started work on a spacecraft that was big enough for ten astronauts and a **cargo bay.**

The cargo bay of this spacecraft could easily hold a satellite.

**A space shuttle looks like an airplane and can land on a runway.**

On April 12, 1981, the first space shuttle was launched. Its crew stayed in space for two days.

# Space Stations

Scientists wanted to know what would happen to people who stayed in space for a long time. They built space stations where **astronauts** could live for months.

**The Mir space station was built during the 1970s.**

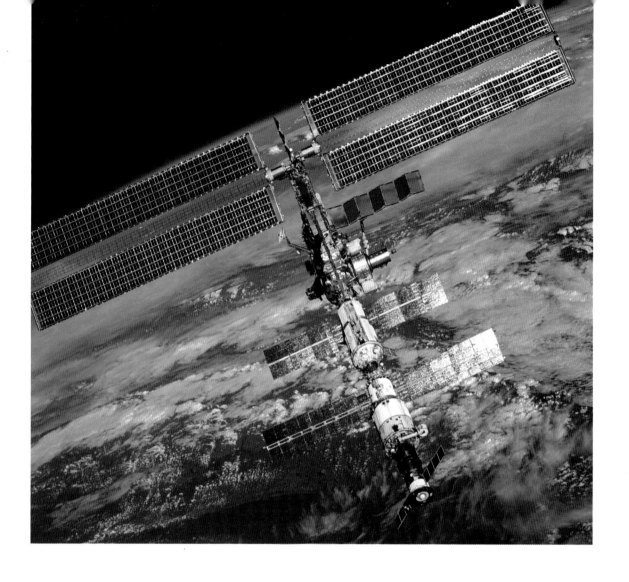

The **Soviets** and Americans built their
own space stations. Then they worked
with fourteen other countries to build the
International Space Station. The first part
of it was launched in November 1998.

To go to Mars and back would take more than two years. **Astronauts** need a way to store enough food and water for the long trip.

26

**Space probes** travel across the solar system, taking pictures and sending them back to Earth along the way. In 1997, a robot named Sojourner landed on Mars. It sent pictures of Mars back to Earth.

# New Ways to Travel?

Scientists keep thinking about new ways to travel into space. One idea is a giant elevator that could take people into space. The elevator would be more than 22,000 miles (35,200 kilometers) high.

This is a drawing of what a space elevator might look like.

**Spacecraft would ride along the rails of the launch arch before launching into space.**

Another new idea for traveling into space is a launch arch to help launch spacecraft. Neither the launch arch or the space elevator has been built yet. It may be many years before they are.

# Amazing Space Facts

- It takes about 10.5 minutes to get to space on board a space shuttle.

- The International Space Station can be seen from Earth. It looks like a tiny point of light moving across the sky.

- Sputnik is Russian for **"satellite."**

- **Astronauts** brought back over 842 pounds (382 kilograms) of rocks from the Moon.

# Glossary

**astronaut**  person who goes to space

**capsule**  part of a rocket that holds astronauts

**cargo bay**  place where satellites and other equipment are stored on a space shuttle

**cosmonaut**  astronaut from the Soviet Union

**experiment**  test

**gravity**  a force that pulls objects together

**lunar module**  part of a space shuttle that lands on the Moon

**Lunar Roving Vehicle**  small car used to travel on the Moon

**satellite**  object that travels around a planet or a moon

**Soviet Union**  the old name for a huge country in Europe and Asia. In 1991, the Soviet Union broke up into separate countries. The largest of these is Russia.

**space probe**  spacecraft used to explore space

## More Books to Read

Whitehouse, Patricia. *The Moon (Space Explorer)*. Chicago: Heinemann Library, 2004.

Whitehouse, Patricia *The Planets (Space Explorer)*. Chicago: Heinemann Library, 2004.

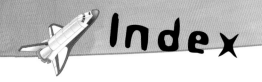

# Index